CONSUMING
FIRE

THE HOPE OF REVIVAL AMONG THE NATIONS

BRIAN BRODERSEN

CALVARY CHAPEL
PUBLISHING

SANTA ANA, CALIFORNIA

Consuming Fire
The Hope of Revival Among the Nations

Published by Calvary Chapel Publishing (CCP)
a resource ministry of Calvary Chapel of Costa Mesa
3800 South Fairview Road
Santa Ana, CA 92704

First printing, 2003

All Scripture quotations in this book, unless otherwise indicated, are taken from the New King James Version. Copyright © 1982, Thomas Nelson, Inc. Used by permission. All rights reserved.

Scripture quotations marked KJV are taken from the King James Version of the Bible.

ISBN 1-931667-70-5

Printed in the United States of America

CONTENTS

INTRODUCTION

Wilt thou not revive us again:
that thy people may rejoice in thee?
Shew us thy mercy, O LORD,
and grant us thy salvation.

Psalm 85:6–7, KJV

Is Another Great Awakening Still Possible?

As we look at the events occurring in the United States and around the world, particularly in the Middle East, we may wonder—where is it all heading? Are we on the brink of another World War as some speculate? Are we about to see the prophecies of Ezekiel 38 and 39 concerning the Islamic invasion of Israel fulfilled? Is the Church about to be raptured, ushering in the judgment of the Great Tribulation?

From a Biblical standpoint, any one or all of these are possible. The world certainly seems ripe for judgment as it attempts to rule God out of its affairs.

Consider the outcry in Britain over the visit of creationist lecturer, Ken Ham. The British press pulled out all the stops in their attack upon Ken Ham and his message.

The Guardian, one of Britain's leading newspapers, published a letter by Professor Niall Shanks of East Tennessee State University, in which he stated this: "If the experience in the United States is anything to go by, this attempt by assorted Christian fundamentalist Taliban-wannabees to turn the clock of science back to the Middle Ages will not stop with biology."[1]

Professor A.C. Grayling from the University of London declared: "… the creation myths are based on nothing but the fantasies of the ignorant who lived long ago … to tell children that ancient traditions, the dreams of our uneducated forefathers, and holy writings which must not be questioned or impugned for fear of blasphemy, are sources of authority about the world on a par with science, is a travesty."[2]

Oxford professor, Richard Dawkins, a great opponent of creationism, stated to the press, "Any science teacher who denies the world is billions (or even millions) of years old is teaching children a preposterous, mind-shrinking falsehood. These men disgrace the honourable profession of teacher."[3]

Finally, one editorial in the *London Times* read, "So long as the antibodies of common sense are all around (as in Britain they are) early exposure to religion can provide a sort of inoculation, and I would personally encourage bands of hooded nuns, creepy evangelists, bearded rabbis and one eyed imams to tour our primary schools wailing incantations and scaring the wits out of kids as a living demonstration of the madness of religion."[4]

This is just an example of the rhetoric coming from many of the journalists and humanistic leaders in Britain. And of course, the outcry in the United States whenever we talk about the subject of creation is very similar. This widespread attack on creationism, and any serious belief in God in general, may cause us to conclude that judgment is inevitable.

Britain is not the only place where hostility to God is becoming commonplace. In April 2002, the United States Supreme Court voted in a six-three decision to protect under the banner of Free Speech certain forms of child pornography. There are numerous cases in United States courts attacking the public display of the Ten Commandments. We may ask ourselves—how much longer can it go on? How much worse can it get? These circumstances could easily lead us to the conclusion that God's patience has run out and judgment is just around the corner. But, there is another possibility, and that is the possibility of revival in the Church and a spiritual awakening in the nation.

It may be hard to believe that a spiritual awakening could happen at this stage, but a quick overview of American history will reveal that as bad as the moral climate is right now, it has been bad in the past.

America has experienced three major spiritual awakenings. They are referred to as "Great Awakenings" because they were movements of the Spirit of God that impacted the very core of the nation and actually altered the course of our history.

We need to remember God's nature and His interaction with men and nations throughout world history.

In addition to the three Great Awakenings, there have been several smaller moves of the Spirit of God that have impacted local areas. Yet, some might say, "We're just too far-gone. There's no way we could see another spiritual awakening in light of the spiritual condition America is in right now!" That might be true, but there are a few things we need to remember when considering whether judgment is imminent or mercy is still possible. We need to remember God's nature and we need to remember His interaction with men and nations throughout world history.

ONE

Judgment Is God's Strange Work

When considering whether judgment is at hand, we need to first remember that according to Isaiah 28:21, judgment is the Lord's strange work. History testifies to the fact that judgment is something God is reluctant to do.

Think of all the wickedness that has marred human history. Think of all the sin and disregard for God and His laws, and how few times God has intervened with judgment. Through the prophet Ezekiel, God said, "I have no pleasure in the death of the wicked" (33:11). When Israel was at the height of wickedness, God would plead with the people and say, "O, turn Israel, turn O backsliding daughter" (see Jeremiah 3:14, 31:22–23). So we see that God is reluctant to judge.

God Delights in Mercy

Second, we need to remember that, according to Micah 7:18, God delights in showing mercy.

One definition of mercy is not getting what one deserves. Now, do we deserve to be judged as a nation? Does the world itself deserve judgment? Absolutely! But, though we deserve it, we cannot finally draw the conclusion that judgment is imminent. It could be that God would choose to show mercy.

Many times in the history of the nation of Israel, it seemed as if they had come to the end; that the people were on the brink of extinction because of their sin. The Book of Judges, for example, covers an approximately 335-year period of time—a time of great moral confusion. Throughout the Book, we are repeatedly told, "In those days there was no king in Israel; everyone did what was right in his own eyes" (Judges 17:6).

Sound familiar? Towards the end of the Book, the fate of the Jews seemed hopeless. It appeared as if nothing could happen to alter the course of Israel's history. Yet, we find that God wasn't finished with His people. The Book of Judges closes with the reign of Samuel as prophet, and ultimately with David ascending to the throne, providing a new day of mercy and grace upon the Jews. So where judgment seemed inevitable, we see that God's intention was to extend mercy to His people.

The history of Judah tells a similar story. Under the reign of Ahaz, an extremely wicked king who turned the Temple in Jerusalem into a place of idolatrous worship, it seemed that life couldn't get any worse for the Jews. However, when Ahaz died, God, in His mercy, raised up Hezekiah, one of the most righteous kings of Judah, and revival broke out. Later, during the reign of Manasseh, a fifty-five-year reign of wickedness, again it seemed that nothing good could come from it. Then Josiah ascended to the throne and through Josiah, God once again brought a time of renewal.

As we follow the history of Israel out to the New Testament period, how much darker could things have gotten than to have Herod the Edomite ruling as king over the Jews at the time of the birth of Christ? This, no doubt, must have seemed like the lowest point in Israel's history. Yet, it was during that dark, dark hour that Jesus Christ came. And following the coming of Jesus Christ was the Day of Pentecost—the single greatest outpouring of God's Spirit upon His people.

Where judgment seemed inevitable, God's intention was to extend mercy to His people.

13

Now if we were to follow history from the Day of Pentecost until the present, considering various regions and nations, we would find similar stories of God's incredible grace and mercy. We see these things illustrated in the history of the United States of America.

America's Forgotten History

The general mindset among Christians today is that until modern times, America was a solidly Christian nation with high moral standards, originally established by godly Founding Fathers, and only recently weakened by the infiltration of humanistic thinking. I believe this somewhat inaccurate view of history can undermine our hope in the possibility of God doing a great work in our day.

You see, if we think it's as bad as it's ever been, and because it's so bad, nothing good can happen in the future, then we are not going to be looking forward in faith to the possibility of God doing something fresh and new in our time. If we concede that all is lost, it is because we don't have a totally accurate view of America's history. Believe it or not, there have been times in the past that were in many ways similar to the times we are living in today.

The Revolutionary period was one of those times. In the late 1700s, many Americans were greatly influenced by the writings of humanists like Voltaire and Rousseau in France, and Thomas Paine and Ethan Allen in America.

Ethan Allen, in his treatise, *Reason, the Only Oracle of Man*, wrote, "... the doctrine of the Trinity is destitute of foundation, and tends manifestly to superstition and idolatry."[5] As to the atonement, Allen declared, "... there could be no justice or goodness in one being's suffering for another, nor is it at all compatible with reason to suppose, that God was the contriver of such a propitiation."[6]

Thomas Paine, in his book, *Age of Reason*, said, "... it is impossible to conceive a story more derogatory to the Almighty, more inconsistent with his wisdom, more contradictory to his power, than this story [the Bible] is."[7] The third President of the United States, Thomas Jefferson was a great admirer of Thomas Paine, and he held to many of the same views.

Finally, a man named Elihu Palmer, who was more or less a disciple of both Paine and Allen, stated in *Principles of Nature*, "The simple truth is, that their pretended Saviour is nothing more than an illegitimate Jew, and their hopes of salvation through him rest on no better foundation than that of fornication or adultery."[8] He went on to say that the Bible is a book, "… whose indecency and immorality shocks all common sense and common honesty."[9] Such was the thinking of the day.

The moral and social conditions at the time of the nation's founding were not as wholesome as we'd like to think. According to the late revival scholar, Dr. J. Edwin Orr, "Drunkenness became epidemic. Out of a population of five million, 300,000 were confirmed drunkards; they were burying fifteen thousand of them each year. Profanity was of the most shocking kind. For the first time in the history of the American settlement, women were afraid to go out at night for fear of assault. Bank robberies were a daily occurrence. …

"The Chief Justice of the United States, John Marshall, wrote to the Bishop of Virginia, James Madison, that the Church 'was too far gone ever to be redeemed.' Voltaire averred, and Tom Paine echoed, 'Christianity will be forgotten in thirty years.' "[10]

Orr reported that colleges were bastions of infidelity. A poll taken at Harvard unearthed the dismal fact that there was not one believer in the whole student body. Princeton boasted only two believers and only five students who didn't belong to the "filthy speech movement" of the day. Students rioted, held a mock communion at William's College, and put on anti-Christian plays at Dartmouth. In New Jersey, students took a Bible from a Presbyterian church and burned it in a public bonfire.

Christians were so few on college campuses in the 1790s that those who did claim allegiance to Christ met in secret and kept their minutes in code so no one would know to whom they belonged.[11] Church historian Kenneth Scott Latourette wrote, "It seemed as if Christianity were about to be ushered out of the affairs of men."[12]

What happened to change things? It was during the 1790s that the Second Great Awakening began. (The First Great Awakening spanned the decades from the 1730s to the 1770s.)

The Second Great Awakening broke out first in Connecticut, and then in Massachusetts and all the seaboard states before spreading to the frontier. A man named James McGready, pastor of three small churches in Logan County, Kentucky, wrote in his diary that the winter of

1799 was a time of "… weeping and mourning with the people of God," while lawlessness prevailed throughout the region. The Great Kentucky Revival began in the summer of 1800. Eleven thousand people came to a communion service.

The modern missionary movement was born out of this Second Great Awakening. Along with it came the abolition of slavery, popular education, Bible societies, Sunday school, and countless other social benefits.[13]

The influence of Christianity upon our national life is not due primarily to our Founding Fathers, although many of them were indeed Christians, but rather to these mighty outpourings of the Spirit of God.

Although the world's circumstances look bleak and it perhaps seems that once again Christianity could be ushered out of the affairs of men, I believe there is the possibility that God in these days might want to work in a special way, pouring out His Spirit, bringing revival to the Church and an awakening to the nations. Both history and the character of God ought to cause us to hope for such things.

Two

What Is Revival?

So, we come to the subject of revival. What is revival? First, let us address what it is not. Revival is not something that we can conjure up ourselves. Perhaps you've driven past a church advertising, "Revival this Week – 7:30 P.M." Revival certainly applies *to* the Church, but it cannot be planned *by* the Church. We don't dictate how and when God will bring about revival. There are things we can do that will lend themselves to revival, but ultimately, it is the sovereign work of God.

Revival has been defined as, "a special season of refreshing when many believers simultaneously experience a deep, Holy Spirit conviction of sin. It results in their confession and renunciation of sin (sometimes publicly). It culminates in a renewal of their dedication to the Lord."[14] Revival leads to a new commitment to holiness, a fresh evangelistic zeal, and a missionary vision.

You see, revival is something God does for His people when we have backslidden and grown cold to the things of the Spirit. Maybe we're still going to church, still carrying around our Bibles, still going through the motions, but in our hearts, we've moved away from that place of intimacy and total commitment to the Lord Jesus Christ.

In *The Spiritual Awakeners*, author Keith Hardman said this about the conditions leading up to revival: "Revival is usually preceded by a time of spiritual depression, apathy, and gross sin, in which the great majority of nominal Christians are hardly different in any substantive way from the members of secular society."[15]

Isn't this the situation we find ourselves in today? Many conversions appear to be taking place, new churches are being started, and in some cases, people are coming in by the droves. When the facts are analyzed closely, however, it becomes clear that, although many churches are filling up with people, the lifestyles of those within the churches and those outside of them are not significantly different. That tells me we need revival!

The Need for Another Great Awakening

An awakening is something that comes alongside revival and impacts those outside the Church, bringing them to a saving faith in Christ. Generally speaking, revival and awakening happen simultaneously. As God begins to move in His Church by His Spirit, bringing a fresh conviction of sin and a fresh call to commitment, God also begins to work in the society outside, convicting people of sin.

Isn't that the great need in our world—for people to come under the conviction of sin? When you talk to people about sin, they dismiss the whole idea, saying, "There's no such thing." How can you convince a person who doesn't believe in absolute truth that truth exists and that all men are in fact sinners?

We need something more than our ability to argue—we need the power of the Spirit of God!

We need something more than our ability to argue—we need the power of the Spirit of God!

Hardman concluded, "Awakenings begin in periods of cultural distortion and grave personal stress, when we lose faith in the legitimacy of our norms, the viability of our institutions, and the authority of our leaders in church and state."[16] Doesn't that describe where we are today? We are ripe for judgment, certainly, but we are also ripe for revival. We are ripe for an awakening. And I believe that as the people of God, we ought to anticipate it.

THREE

Reasons to Hope

Mercy—God's Delight

There are three reasons why I believe that we should hope for revival.

First, God delights in showing mercy. He takes pleasure in it. He enjoys it.

Sometimes when I'm praying for revival and for God to show mercy on this sin-sick world, I find myself thinking, "Lord, You ought to just judge this planet!" But then I have to stop and remember, "I was just like these people."

You could say the same thing. We were just like them at one time, living for ourselves, having no regard for God or the things of God. Not the slightest bit interested, living in sin, rebelling against God, and frankly not really caring about any of it at all. Yet what did God do? He extended mercy to us. Amazing!!! So, because God delights in showing mercy, we as God's people ought to anticipate that perhaps at this dark hour, He might still choose to graciously pour out His Spirit.

The Promised Outpouring of the Spirit

Second, I believe that we should hope for revival because the Scripture speaks of the Spirit being poured out in the last days. This promise is found repeatedly in the Bible. "In the last days, I will pour My Spirit on all flesh, says the LORD" (see Joel 2:28). And so, we can Biblically anticipate outpourings of the Spirit of God as we get closer and closer to the coming of the Lord Jesus Christ.

Unfinished Business

The third reason I believe we should hope for revival (and this is purely subjective) is because it seems that God is moving in that direction. Although there are many things that appear to point in the direction of the Second Coming—whether it be international situations or the Middle East crisis—as I look at other events, I get the sense that there is still something that God is going to accomplish before Jesus returns.

I believe this because of my own experience of what God is doing in and through the ministry of Calvary Chapel. I am not saying that Calvary Chapel is the only ministry through which God is moving today. He's working through many ministries, and we thank God for that. But I'm not involved in those other ministries so I don't know the details. I do know the details, however, of what He's doing with Calvary Chapel. And as I look at what He is accomplishing through the ministry of Calvary Chapel, it seems that the Lord is moving, and He is preparing to do something significant in the future.

As a ministry, we've grown to over one thousand affiliated churches in the United States and hundreds more internationally. Weekly we get stacks of applications for affiliation. New churches are being planted, and men are being raised up to spread the Gospel. People want to be part of what God is doing in and through Calvary Chapel.

We have the Bible colleges and extension campuses both in the States and overseas where literally thousands of young men and women are preparing themselves for service to God. I look at that and think, "Okay, Lord, it looks like this is all preparatory for something in the future."

When I first went into Europe many years ago, our ministry was limited to evangelizing on the streets and meeting in people's homes. Today, we have conference centers and Bible Colleges in England, Germany, Austria, and Hungary, as well as new churches emerging monthly. Now, I look at all of this and think, "Lord, You have laid the groundwork, You have laid a foundation. It is hard for me to believe that You would have laid the foundation without intending to erect the structure." " 'Shall I bring to the time of birth, and not cause delivery?' Says the LORD" (Isaiah 66:9a).

I look at the expansion of our radio ministry—not only are we broadcasting Bible teaching all over the United States, but also all over Europe, Australia, New Zealand, and various parts of Africa! Every day people all over the world contact us to say, "This radio station has revolutionized my life." And they're going back to their churches—not Calvary Chapel churches necessarily, but Lutheran, Anglican, Presbyterian, Baptist, or Catholic churches—saying, "God has really touched me through this radio station." They are encouraging people to tune in. God is doing something, and again, I see that and think, "Well, Lord, it seems peculiar that You would build all of this up, only to pull the plug."

I could be dead wrong. But, because of what I see happening in our own ministry, I am convinced we ought to be hoping and praying for revival and spiritual awakening. Is a fresh outpouring of God's Spirit guaranteed? Can we say dogmatically, authoritatively, "If we do A, B, and C, then God is obligated to bring about revival?" Let me quote A.W. Tozer to answer that question:

"Let any man turn to God in earnest ... and the results will exceed anything he may have hoped [for] in his leaner and weaker days."

"What God in His sovereignty may yet do on a world-scale I do not claim to know. But what He will do for the plain man or woman who seeks His face I believe I do know and can tell others. Let any man turn to God in earnest, let him begin to exercise himself unto godliness, let him seek to develop his powers of spiritual receptivity by trust and obedience and humility, and the results will exceed anything he may have hoped [for] in his leaner and weaker days."[17]

FOUR

Creating a Spark

Is there a worldwide awakening coming? Could a national revival be just around the corner? I don't know. But this I do know: A personal revival will take place in any man or woman who says, "Jesus, be Lord of all." For some people, their prayer might be expressed this way: "Lord, I want to get back to where I was in those early days as a Christian. I want that passion and that fire. I want You to be the priority in my life once again." Revival will come for us individually if we seek Him. And inevitably, if it comes for us individually, it's going to touch others.

There have been Great Awakenings and there have been lesser moves of the Spirit, not necessarily impacting the whole nation or the world, but impacting certain regions. So it is possible that you might have a Los Angeles or New York City revival; or, a London, Tokyo, or Beijing revival. Revival could start in some obscure place and spread around the world. You never know what God might do!

Personal revival is indeed guaranteed. So where does it start? It starts with you and me. It starts with our determination to get right with God completely. We can pray:

"God, if there's anything that has come into my life that's not of You, then I pray You would remove it. And God, if there's anything lacking in my life that You want to instill, I pray You would bring it."

If you pray that sincerely, God will do it, and revival will begin.

The Welsh revival of 1904–1905 began with a young woman named Florrie Evans publicly proclaiming, "I love the Lord Jesus with all my heart." A few months later, over one hundred thousand people from all walks of life were proclaiming the same thing. The initial spark, however, was one newly

A personal revival will take place in any man or woman who says, "Jesus, be Lord of all."

converted young woman standing up in a meeting in absolute purity and sincerity, expressing what had happened within her: "I love the Lord Jesus with all my heart." That sparked a fire and changed the course of history for many people. Not only was Wales transformed, but many other nations were as well because that powerful move of the Spirit spread out from there.[18]

This is the searching question to consider: Do you love Jesus Christ with all your heart? Can you affirm that? Not around your peers, not to impress anyone publicly, but standing alone before God, can you affirm, "I love Jesus Christ with all of my heart"? Can you say honestly, "Lord, to the best of my knowledge and to the best of my ability, I am completely sold out to You and committed to doing Your will"? If you cannot say that with conviction, then I suggest you need revival.

The Urgency of the Matter

As we look out at our world we often wonder, how bad is it going to get? We ask, "Is there anything we can do to bring about a significant change in our society?" Some people emphasize the need for social reform and political involvement. As helpful as that can sometimes be, we need more. We need a drastic change in our culture. The only way we will see such a transformation is if large numbers of people have a radical change of heart. And the only one who can re-make a heart is Jesus Christ! Here's the good news: He's doing that!

We are presently seeing growing numbers of young people who, not that long ago, were caught up in the party scene. Some of them were into drugs, alcohol, and sexual immorality; others were just wasting their time, sitting around listening to music, watching movies, and basically entertaining themselves to death. But something is happening. God is moving! Now these young people are gathering together and instead of filling their minds with the perverse ramblings of some dead cultural icon, they've got their Bibles out, they're sharing Scriptures with each other, they're worshipping the Lord, they're writing their own music, and they're praying that God would touch their friends. And, He's doing it! All of this tells me God is on the move, and I believe that there are greater things to come.

FIVE

Hoping for Brighter Days

Lighting the Match

Now that we have established that God is reluctant to judge and is anxious to show mercy; and history—particularly that of Israel and our own nation—provides encouragement for the possibility of revival and awakening in the future, let's consider the steps we as Christians must take if we are to have any hope of brighter days ahead.

In II Chronicles chapter 7, verse 14, God Himself outlines what could be called "The Steps to Revival." God shows us what to do when conditions develop as they have in our time: "If My people who are called by My name will humble themselves, and pray and seek My face, and turn from their wicked ways, then I will hear from heaven, and will forgive their sin and heal their land."

This is probably one of the most misapplied texts in all the Bible. On several occasions, I have heard people apply this text to the United States, implying that we as a country are the people of God, and we need to turn back to Him. But that isn't an accurate application of the passage because God was speaking to Israel and Israel was a theocracy—a nation or kingdom under the direct rule of God. Israel was really the one and only theocracy the world has ever known. So even though the United States of America was built upon Christian principles and founded by men who were, for the most part, professing Christians, it wouldn't be totally accurate to say that we are a Christian nation.

Therefore, the instruction in II Chronicles does not apply to the United States, or to any other country in a geographic or geopolitical sense, but rather it applies to the Church, which Peter calls a "Holy Nation" (I Peter 2:9). We, the Church, are His people, called by His name. So this is a message for us. If we want to see a fresh work of God in our midst and an overflow into our society, we have to take these steps ourselves. It begins with us.

There are four steps to revival, according to this passage.

Acknowledgment of Sin

Let's look at the first step: "If My people will humble themselves ..." What the Lord is really talking about is the acknowledgment of *our* sin. There is a human tendency, and I don't think that we as Christians are completely free from it, to point the finger at others and to blame them for our troubles.

Quite often, I hear Christians say things like: "Oh, it's the government's fault that we are in this moral mess today. It's our political leaders who have departed from those godly principles upon which our nation was founded." Others say, "The liberal media and the constant barrage of liberal ideas are corrupting the country. Hollywood is the culprit. The entertainment industry is bringing us down. They're the ones polluting the world."

I personally would agree that every one of these factors, and a few others as well, are contributing to the problem of moral corruption and spiritual decline in our country. But, what we need to admit is that we, ourselves, are not without fault. We have failed. We have not been the people that we should be. I have to look at myself honestly and say, "Many times I haven't been the godly man that I ought to be. I have to admit that I haven't always sought the Lord with all my heart. I haven't devoted myself totally and completely to Him as I ought to. I have to recognize that I'm guilty." We have to recognize that we are guilty! That's where real change begins. God said, "If My people ... will humble themselves ..."

We seem to have an inbred tendency to overlook our own sin. The Laodicean Christians illustrate this point well. Their evaluation of themselves was—we are rich, increased with goods, and in need of nothing. Jesus' perspective was a direct contrast to theirs. He said, "You are wretched, miserable, poor, blind, and naked" (see Revelation 3:17). You see how easy it is to fool ourselves?

We have to recognize that we are guilty! That's where real change begins.

Consider David. He had committed the horrific sin of adultery, then compounded it by sending Bathsheba's husband to the front lines in battle so that he would die. David had sinned so horribly, yet he went about his business as king and as the spiritual leader of Israel, suppressing that conviction of sin, trying to pretend nothing was wrong in his life—until Nathan the prophet came to him with a parable.

Nathan tells David a story about a great injustice that has taken place—a wealthy man has taken advantage of a poor man. The rich man has a huge flock; the poor man has only one little lamb that is like a child to him. When a guest arrives at the home of the rich man, instead of going to his own flock and picking out a lamb that he might prepare a meal, he takes the only lamb that the poor man owns. Not realizing it's a parable, David becomes outraged that such an injustice could occur within his kingdom. He explodes, "That man shall die!" Nathan turns to him and says, "David, you are the man."

You see, David was blind to his own state. He was quick to point the finger and pronounce judgment, but he was blind to his own condition. Clearly, David was a true man of God because when Nathan's words pierced his conscience, he humbled himself that instant. He said, "I have sinned." But we see in David the same tendency we all have to point the finger away from ourselves.

Think of Isaiah the prophet in the early stages of his ministry. He went about pronouncing woe upon the nation of Israel. It's intriguing, when reading the first five chapters of Isaiah, to find how many times he pronounced judgment upon the people. He said, "Woe unto the wicked. Woe unto those who rise early to follow after strong drink. Woe unto those who draw iniquity with cords of deceit. Woe unto those who call evil good and good evil. Woe unto those who are wise in their own eyes." Isaiah travelled throughout the kingdom pronouncing these judgments upon the sinners in the land.

Then we come to the sixth chapter, and an interesting thing happens. We read, "In the year that king Uzziah died," Isaiah said, "*I* saw the LORD. He was sitting upon the throne. He was high and lifted up. And the train of His robe filled the temple with glory. And the cherubim were crying, 'Holy, Holy, Holy.' " And then Isaiah said, "Woe is *me*" (Isaiah 6:5, italics added). Isaiah was quick to pronounce woe upon everyone except himself. Then, he sees the Lord and he is a changed man.

If we can't see our own faults and the contribution that we've made to the moral decline within our society, it's probably because we haven't seen the Lord. Because the moment we see Him, like Isaiah, we must cry out, "Woe is me, I am undone! Because, I am a man of unclean lips" (Isaiah 6:5).

One man who should not have been implicated in the sins of his people was Daniel. He was an exceptional, godly man. As you read the account of his life, you will be hard-pressed to find any inconsistencies. And yet even Daniel included himself as he prayed, saying, "Lord, we have sinned." He didn't say, "Lord, they have sinned, get them!" He said, "Lord, we have sinned."

Like Daniel, we too must start with our own sins, with our own shortcomings, and with the fact that we have not really lived up to God's calling upon our lives. This is where it all begins: "If My people who are called by My name will humble themselves ..." We need to come to God honestly, asking, "Search me, O God, and know my heart; try me, and know my anxieties; and see if there is any wicked way in me" (Psalm 139: 23–24a).

I am certain that, as we ask, God will bring to our attention areas in our lives that are out of sync with what He wants to do and what He has called us to be.

Repentance

The next step that is laid out for us in II Chronicles is the step of repentance. "If My people who are called by My name will ... turn from their wicked ways." You see, it is not good enough to acknowledge that we are in sin; we must turn away from our sins as well.

We are living in a time when sin dominates the lives of many Christians. Sin is rampant in the Church today—not just the Catholic Church, which is presently getting all the publicity—but the Evangelical Church is full of sin as well.

In 2002, Barna Research Group reported that less than half of all born again Christians in America rely on the Bible as their primary source for moral guidance. Thirty-three percent say it is morally acceptable to view sexually explicit television, movies, and Internet, while forty percent say reading magazines depicting graphic sexuality and nudity is OK. A significant number believe that living together and divorce apart from adultery are OK. One-out-of-five think abortion is morally acceptable. And, two-thirds of those who said they tithed their income were found to have lied when their finances were examined.[19]

Something grievous has happened in that we have developed a high tolerance for sin in our generation. The Evangelical Church has become polluted with idolatry, sexual immorality, divorce, hatred, jealousy, selfish ambition, slander, and gossip.

Idolatry

Consider idolatry, for example. Now you might say, "Wait a second, we don't have any statues around here. I don't have any images that I bow down to. What do you mean idolatry?" Well, you see, idolatry is manifested in many ways. Bowing down to images is just one of those ways. Idolatry is a matter of the heart. A person becomes idolatrous when he or she allows something other than God to take the primary place in their life.

It is not good enough to acknowledge that we are in sin; we must turn away from our sins as well.

As Pastor Chuck Smith has said many times, "The master passion of your life becomes your God." If the Lord is your master passion, then you are right where you ought to be. But if something else is your master passion, if something else has taken over and is driving you, then you are caught up in idolatry. Three manifestations of idolatry common in our generation are: (1) the love of self, (2) the love of things, and (3) the love of pleasure.

Many people, even Christians, are caught up in one, two, or all three of these. The love of self is the attitude that says, "It's all about me." Maybe you don't come out and verbalize this type of idolatry because you know it would bring a lightening bolt upon your head. But, you conduct your life as if it's all about you. Everything revolves around you, what you want, your agenda. Basically, you are on the throne of your life and for you to utter the words "Lord Jesus" is a contradiction. You are calling Him Lord, but you are not obeying Him. You are doing your own thing instead of His will.

Then there is the love of things: I want this, or I have to get that. Living in an affluent culture, we can easily get caught up in the love of things. As we begin to get the things we want, so often a vicious cycle begins, and we no longer have time to devote ourselves entirely to the Lord because we have to devote ourselves to our three jobs so we can get more things! That is idolatry.

Materialism is idolatry. We don't talk about materialism too much. It's taboo. We don't want to offend the rich, but many people in the Church conduct themselves by the philosophy of living for things and loving pleasure.

The Sensual Delusion

For others, what feels good is all that matters. Sexual immorality is rampant in the Church today. Adultery is becoming commonplace, and not just within the congregation. Quite often, the pastors in the pulpit are the ones involved in adulterous relationships.

We have lost the understanding of the seriousness of the sin of adultery. Remember that under the Old Covenant, adultery was a capital crime, punishable by death. God has not changed His mind about adultery. So why do we tolerate it in the Church so readily? I'm afraid we have convinced ourselves that God is nothing more than a glorified psychologist who understands that we have "needs" and who has nothing but our personal happiness as His top priority. What a sad and tragic delusion!

Fornication is as offensive to God as adultery. Fornication is sexual activity outside the marriage relationship. In our churches today, we have people involved with one another sexually, but not committed to one another in marriage. Again, many times, this issue is swept under the carpet.

We are living in such a distorted time spiritually that we have even renamed these grievous sins "psychological disorders." We can read about "sex addicts" who have gone off to the Christian psychologist and been told that they are not really responsible for the adultery or the fornication because they happen to be the unfortunate victim of a sexual addiction. "We'll help you through therapy and medication," they say, "but you'll have to live with this disease for the rest of your life." As pathetic as it sounds, many Christians are buying into this psychobabble.

Then, of course, there is the plague of pornography which, no doubt, contributes to the fornication and adultery within the Church. Again, we have to take a look at ourselves. We are always blaming the people in the pornography industry, and judgment will certainly come upon them, but who is buying the stuff from them? Who's surfing the Net and going to those sites? Unfortunately, many Christians are caught up in this filth, and sometimes, sad to say, so are the leaders in the Church.

Divorce—The Acceptable Sin

Next, we come to the great and grievous sin of divorce. As we've seen, many Christians don't believe divorce is a sin. We are almost afraid to talk about divorce as a sin today. In some cases, preachers are afraid to mention divorce from their pulpits for fear that half the church will leave. They fail to remember God's Word, which says, "He hates divorce" (Malachi 2:16).

When I talk about the sin of divorce, I want to clarify what I mean. There are certain circumstances under which divorce is allowed by God. Some were divorced before becoming Christians. Others are divorced because their spouse was unfaithful. Still others, women primarily, have had to flee for their lives because of an abusive spouse. Lastly, divorce might have occurred because an unbelieving spouse decided to leave their believing husband or wife. I am not talking about any of these situations.

Who I am talking about are those who have no Biblical basis for divorce—those who say things like, "My husband doesn't really meet my needs anymore, therefore the Lord has freed me from my marriage." Do you know how many times we as pastors hear rationalizations like this in counseling sessions? Far too many! Or we hear a man say, "Because my wife no longer satisfies me, the Lord has released me from my marriage." The Bible makes it clear that if a person divorces their spouse for any reason except sexual immorality, he or she has committed adultery.

Divorce is one of those sins that has brought a major blight upon the Church. There is a huge need for repentance in this area. The Lord cannot bless the church that turns a blind eye to this grievous sin.

These are just a few of the many sins that are grieving and quenching the Spirit's work in our midst. If we hope to see brighter days ahead for the Church, we must repent! If there is any hope for our nation, it has to begin in our churches. It has to begin in our own lives. We have got to humble ourselves and repent. We have to turn from our wicked ways.

Total Devotion

Third, God says in II Chronicles, "If My people will seek My face ..." This is a way of describing someone who is pursuing God, someone who has an intense passion for Him, someone who is going after God with all of his or her heart. What God is talking about is total devotion.

Practically speaking, how do we seek His face? We do it by being in His Word. The Bible is the means through which God reveals Himself to us. So in our devotion to Him, in our seeking of His face, we are going to be spending much of our time in the Scriptures— reading and meditating upon them.

The Bible is to be the rallying point for the Christian Church. It is the place of meeting between God and the individual Christian. If I am seeking God's face, it is going to be manifested by the fact that the Bible is a priority in my life. Millions and millions of books have been written, but there is *only one Book* in the world that is the inspired, inerrant, authoritative Word of God, and that is the Bible. We, of all people, in all of history, are the most privileged because we have more access to the Bible than any generation before us! But along with this privilege comes great responsibility.

If there is any hope for our nation, it has to begin in our churches. It has to begin in our own lives.

Some years ago, a man wrote a book entitled, *Sodom Had No Bible*. The implication was that if God judged Sodom, which had no Bibles to teach the people right from wrong, the truth about God, the way of salvation and so on, what greater judgment will He bring upon those countries that have free access to the Bible, yet neglect or disobey it? It is a great privilege to have a Bible, and God expects us to take that privilege seriously.

If I am seeking God's face, it is going to be manifested by the fact that the Bible is a priority in my life.

We need to bring the Scriptures to bear upon every aspect of our lives—our families, our jobs, and our ministries. Our great passion and desire can and should center on the Word of God.

In the beginning stages of the Calvary Chapel movement, it was common for people to bring their Bibles to church as they do today. The difference was that people were also found throughout their communities carrying their Bibles with them, reading and discussing them publicly. I believe God wants to inspire a similar passion in us again.

We are called to seek God's face. Bible reading and meditation—personally and corporately—are ways of seeking His face, particularly when we do it in a worshipful rather than a mechanical manner.

Prayer

The fourth and final step is prayer. "If My people will pray ..." Prayer is one of the greatest privileges of the Christian's life. It is also one of the most neglected. Prayer is nothing less than direct access to the God of the universe. Sometimes as I look around at the moral disintegration in our society, I think, "If I could just get to somebody at the top and talk to him ... If I could just share my views with the President, or perhaps I could go before Congress with my concerns, or maybe I could get an audience with the Queen or the Prime Minister." But, as we all know, that kind of thing rarely happens. Even if I did get that opportunity, there is no guarantee that anything would actually change.

In contrast, we as Christians have the incredible privilege of going to God—the Maker and Sustainer of everything, the Governor of the whole universe—and saying to Him, "Lord, did

You see that? Do You see what's going on there? Lord, what do You think about that? We should do something about that, shouldn't we, Lord?"

Then God gives us direction and He begins to work. What a privilege we possess! Tragically, we neglect that great privilege. The prayer meeting is the most sparsely attended meeting at most churches today.

History tells us about the importance of prayer in regard to spiritual awakening. In a booklet entitled *The Role of Prayer in Spiritual Awakening*, Dr. J. Edwin Orr wrote the following: "In September 1857, a man of prayer, Jeremiah Lanphier, started a prayer meeting in the upper room of the Dutch Reformed Church Consistory Building, in Manhattan. In response to his advertisement, only six people out of the population of a million showed up. But, the following week, there were fourteen, and then twenty-three, when it was decided to meet every day for prayer. By late winter, they were filling the Dutch Reformed Church, then the Methodist Church on John Street, then Trinity Episcopal Church on Broadway at Wall Street. In February and March of 1858, every church and public hall in downtown New York was filled.

"Horace Greeley, the famous editor, sent a reporter with horse and buggy racing around the prayer meetings to see how many men were praying: in one hour, he could get to only twelve meetings, but he counted 6,100 men attending. Then a landslide of prayer began, which overflowed to the churches in the evenings. People began to be converted, ten thousand a week in New York City alone. The movement spread throughout New England, the church bells bringing people to prayer at eight in the morning, twelve noon, six in the evening. … More than a million people were converted to God in one year out of a population of thirty million."[20]

I came across an article in an out-of-print publication, which stated the following: "In 1904 a group of missionaries became deeply concerned that the Church had not been established in [Korea] in the way God longed for it to be. Korea had been known as the 'Hermit Kingdom,' literally folding her mountains about herself and warding off any infiltration of Western ideas or religions. Only in subtle ways, such as through medicine or schools, could the Gospel be preached. Consequently, there began noonday prayer meetings. Missionaries of every mission station in Korea, by common consent, knelt for one hour to pray for victory in that land.

"After a couple of months, a missionary at one of the stations spoke up. We will call him an efficiency expert … and we have plenty of them. He said, 'We have been praying for a long time, but have seen nothing radical happen. I would suggest that to save time we dispense of these noon meetings and pray privately at our own devotions for revival in Korea.'

"But another missionary gave a quick response. 'I believe God has not answered our prayers because we are not praying enough. I recommend we continue these noon meetings and spend an hour in the evening as well.' The plan was adopted unanimously. Word got around to other mission stations and soon every mission group in Korea was spending two hours a day in prayer for revival in that land. In a matter of weeks a lightening bolt of revival struck and like a rolling prairie fire went the length and breadth of Korea.

"More than fifty thousand converts were added to the Church."[21]

Isn't that incredible?! But what has happened in the past is just a promise of what God will do in the future *if* we will take the steps towards revival and *if* we will begin to pray for it to come. Consider this—what if we decide, corporately, to set aside an hour a day to pray that God would pour out His Spirit? And what if we commit to getting together one evening a week with a couple of friends to pray and just to begin asking God to pour out His Spirit?

I'll tell you what will happen. God will pour out His Spirit. As we read in II Chronicles 7, when we have followed these steps to revival, God says, "Then I will hear from heaven, and will forgive their sin and heal their land." God promises to respond as we take His call seriously.

Six

A World Aflame

Maybe, Maybe Not

Is personal revival going to result in a worldwide revival? We don't know. Will it ultimately transform our national life? We can't be certain. But of this we can be sure: Personal revival will result in the transformation of our lives, and it will result in the transformation of lives around us as well. It will result in the transformation and restoration of families. It will instill a fresh sense of God's presence in our churches. And as that begins to happen, it will flow over to our communities, and they will be transformed. Then perhaps God might move things out, touching the whole nation and going around the world.

The great revivals throughout history have not been isolated to one location. As each revival grew, it would start in one place and move out from there. Simultaneous outpourings of the

Spirit of God were seen in various places all over the world.

Revival has to start somewhere, and it can start with us. Matthew Henry said, "When God intends great mercy for his people the first thing he does is to set them a praying."[22]

Do you remember the situation back in the time of Elijah the prophet? There was a great drought upon the land both literally and spiritually. When Elijah came to Ahab, king of Israel, after three-and-a-half years of drought, he said, "I hear the sound of an abundance of rain" (see I Kings 18:41). Although he was speaking literally, I believe there is a spiritual lesson intended as well, as oftentimes in the Scripture rain and water speak symbolically of the Holy Spirit.

Revival has to start somewhere, and it can start with us.

When Elijah said, "I hear the sound of an abundance of rain," there wasn't a cloud in the sky. But as he continued to pray, it says in verse 44 that there appeared a cloud the size of a man's hand. Elijah then said, "Tell Ahab to come down from Mount Carmel because a storm is coming."

And it wasn't long before that little cloud, the size of a man's hand, turned into a downpour that soaked the land and brought life back to the nation.

Oh, how we need an abundance of that same spiritual rain upon the Church and our land today. May God in His abundant mercy open the windows of heaven and pour upon us blessings we can't contain! Amen.

DR. J. EDWIN ORR

History of Revival

*[Note to the reader: every attempt has been made to maintain
the historical accuracy of the events and people described herein
as reported by Dr. Orr. However, we were unable to confirm some
names and places.]*

In Philadelphia, there was a little book
published—*Pentecost*, or *The Work of God in
Philadelphia*—describing the impact of the Great
Awakening of 1858 in that city. The moderator
of the Irish Presbyterian Church and another
minister crossed the Atlantic to bring fraternal
greetings to the American Presbyterians, and
they were deeply impressed with what they saw
of the Great Awakening in Pennsylvania. They
republished the little booklet in Ireland and
people began praying for revival in Ireland.

Now, of course, Ireland is a Roman Catholic
country, but there is a strong minority of
Protestants in the north. These people began
praying for revival. Many sermons were preached
on the subject. Many prayer meetings were
started. The first of the prayer meetings seemed to
be one begun in Kells near Ballymena by a young
man called James McQuilkin. He'd been reading

the testimony of George Müller, the great saint of faith who ran the orphanage in Bristol. And then he heard of the revival in America, so he said to himself, "If God answers prayer, why shouldn't we expect such a work of God in Ireland also?" He asked God to give him some other young men to join with him in prayer and soon they met, four of them, in a barn outside Kells near Ballymena. Their names, if I remember rightly, were James McQuilkin, Jeremiah Meneely, Robert Carlisle, and John Wallace.

Now this little prayer meeting of four young men increased. They were invited on the fourteenth of March, 1859, to speak in the First Presbyterian Church in the town of Ahoghill. There was such a large crowd attending that it was deemed prudent to dismiss the meeting lest there be a fatal accident from the falling in of the galleries. Whereupon the laymen stood in the church portico and preached to three thousand people in the streets. Many began falling to their knees. It was sleet at that time—rain and snow—but people who were moved by the powerful preaching of the laymen fell to their knees on the muddy street. This was the first outbreak of mass conviction in the United Kingdom at that time.

Now just three miles away was the town of Ballymena, and it had a population of about six thousand, largely Presbyterian. The Ballymena newspaper noted the revival on the twenty-sixth of March and began chronicling the events.

A number of prepared young laymen devoted almost all of their time to helping in the revival because most of the ministers were away south in Dublin at annual meetings. But in the month of May 1859, the awakening made its first appearance in Belfast, a busy city of 120,000. One-third of them were Roman Catholic. But before the end of May, the Belfast newspapers were giving half of a column or a column of news to the great revival that began in that city. The attendances went up from twenty-five thousand to forty thousand.

With something like unanimity, the ministers of Belfast started a united prayer meeting in the music hall with the mayor in the chair. A week later, Dr. Knox, the Bishop of the United Dioceses of Down, Connor, and Dromore, took the chair, assisted by 146 ministers of all denominations, including the moderator of the General Assembly and the president of the Wesleyan Methodist Conference. Now the revival was underway in the north of Ireland.

Out of a population of less than one million, one hundred thousand people were converted. One of the strange features of this revival as distinct from the American revival of 1858 was that many people were violently prostrated. They collapsed. At that time, it was called being slain in the Spirit. It was a little bit different than what is talked about nowadays because these were not seekers but often sinners that were prostrated.

The revival spread throughout the whole of Ireland. Before the middle of summer, they were having twenty thousand at prayer meetings in the botanic gardens. The October attendance at the Maze Racecourse attracted only five hundred people instead of ten thousand. A large distillery capable of turning out one million gallons of whiskey annually was put up for auction. These were the reports that were confirmed by the Evangelical Alliance meeting in Belfast at that time.

This was supported by all denominations. The great movement spread across to Scotland. The population of Scotland at that time was about three million. Out of the three million, three hundred thousand were converted. The General Assembly of the Church of Scotland noticed in its meetings in Edinburgh, May 1860, "The General

Assembly, taking into consideration the gratifying evidence manifested in many countries, and in various districts of our own land, of an increased anxiety about salvation and deepening interest in religious ordinances, followed in so many cases by the fruits of holy living, desires to record its gratitude to Almighty God. ..."

The General Assembly of the Free Church of Scotland passed a similar resolution, which described it as a "mighty rushing wind throughout the country." The same thing happened with the United Presbyterians. These three branches of the dominant Presbyterians of Scotland, who accounted for about seventy percent of the population, all supported this great revival spreading throughout Scotland in 1859.

The explanation? Prayer, I would say. Here's a report: the United Presbyterian Church reported that 1-in-every-4 of its 162,305 communicants were attending private prayer meetings—an average of 40,549 at prayer in 1,205 regular meetings, with 129 new prayer meetings, and 16,362 new attendees in 1859. So one has to agree that the revival began with prayer.

Revival came to Glasgow, the great Scottish city, with the suddenness of a thunderstorm in summer. A column was devoted to a public meeting held in the city hall to describe what was happening in Ireland, not too far away. And then suddenly, August 19, a public meeting was held in Glasgow Green, with twenty thousand people attending. This revival spread through every part of Scotland. Here's the sort of report we get about the times of refreshing in Glasgow:

> Every Sabbath evening service, since the Bridegate Church was opened, the crowds around the stone pulpit have been increasing.

(I should stop to explain. They had built a pulpit outside the church because people couldn't get into the church.)

> Until last Sabbath evening, there could not have been fewer than seven thousand hearers. The voice of the preacher appeared to be perfectly audible at the furthest extremity. At the close of the open-air-service, an invitation was given from the pulpit to all who wished to come to decision in the matter of religion to attend a prayer meeting. Within ten minutes the church was packed, upwards of eleven hundred when thus crowded.

In other words, they did the preaching in the open air outside the church and used the church as an inquiry room. This was happening in every part of Scotland. It spread up through the Highlands and the islands. The Reverend W.T. Ker of Deskford said, "It is indeed a most wondrous work of the Lord, and it is passing along this whole coast like a mighty wave, having assumed a character identical to the work in Ireland."

Now the revival continued year after year. It was summed up about six years after it, "The wave of Divine blessing came to us apparently from Ireland four or five years ago. It struck first the west coast of Scotland, then spread over a great part of the country. It was a very blessed season, perhaps the most extensive operation we've ever known among us."

Now this same revival broke out in Wales, independent of the Irish revival. At that time, Wales was largely Welsh speaking. I came across some reports of a man called Humphrey Jones, who led revival in New York State among the Welsh settlers. He came back to spread the Good News to Wales. He started to preach in a town called Ysbytty Ystwyth. There the Presbyterian minister went to hear him but wasn't much impressed with anything that was derived from America or from the Methodists. But when he preached on, "Because thou art lukewarm and neither cold nor hot, I will spit you out of my mouth," David Morgan, the Presbyterian, was deeply convicted and became the great evangelist of the Welsh Revival. Again, about one hundred thousand people were converted in Wales.

The revival impacted every county in Wales. It began among the Welsh-speaking people, but it spread to the English-speaking and greatly stirred Cardiff, the capital of Wales. The revival continued in Wales year after year and people have summed it up for us in their reports.

Now the same revival began in northern England; it broke out in Newcastle-on-Tyne. The Reverend Robert Young, who was president of the Methodist Conference, said, "The revival with which this town is favoured is advancing with increased power and glory. In Brunswick Place Chapel, we hold a united prayer meeting from twelve o'clock to one; another meeting for exhortation and prayer from three to five; and a similar service from seven to ten. Many seem 'filled with the Holy Ghost' and pray 'as the Spirit gives them utterance.' "

The revival spread throughout the whole of the north. Just south of Newcastle-on-Tyne is Gateshead, and there a young Methodist minister caught fire and became a fiery evangelist. In fact, his church was called "The Converting Shop." People were so scared to go there; they didn't go unless they wanted to be converted, sure of being converted if they went. The name of the young minister was William Booth, and he and his wife, Catherine, became evangelists for the next ten years until they founded the Salvation Army.

Now the revival spread throughout the Midlands and throughout the south. Early in 1860, a London lady named Mrs. Elizabeth Codner published anonymously a poem whose sentiments expressed so sincerely the feeling of the Revival movements already underway in Ulster and Scotland and Wales:

> "Lord, I hear of showers of blessing
>   Thou art scattering full and free;
> Showers on thirsty land refreshing;
>   Let some dropping fall on me,
>   Even me."

They had a great meeting in North London in the Islington Hall. The second week of

January was devoted to prayer throughout the whole country and then revival began spreading throughout London.

All the churches were filled. At that time they had great evening services at St. Paul's Cathedral, led by the Bishop of London, and great services in Westminster Abbey led by the Dean of Westminster. But where did the poor people go? The churches couldn't hold them. They went to the theatres, all the famous theatres. The Britannia, the Garrick, the Sadler's Wells Theatres, and Covent Garden Theatre were filled each Sunday evening with crowds of people. The aggregate attendance nightly was 20,000, and I suppose one could say that an aggregate of 865,000 attended one theatre alone—the Victoria Theatre in Waterloo.

The revival spread throughout London. Spurgeon built his tabernacle in London at that time. The Baptists added twenty percent to their sittings in London.

The revival spread to other parts of Southern England and became, of course, the event of the century at that particular time. The difference was that in Britain there was some opposition to the revival as compared to the United States.

The Church of England had five distinct parties. First of all, the old fashioned High Church people; second, the Tractarians representing an Anglo-Catholic revival; third, the Broad Church people, who weren't too particular about doctrine; fourth, the Simonite Low Church people; and lastly, the very strong Evangelicals. The strong Evangelicals of the Church of England supported the revival from the beginning. The Low Church people generally supported it, but not all of them. The Broad Church people were not interested, and the High Church people were opposed to it. But the Baptists, the Methodists, and other denominations throughout England were in strong support of that revival.

I've estimated the number of conversions in seven years to exceed one million. It's rather difficult to get statistics from a state church which doesn't keep statistics of conversions, but I estimate from all the figures that the total number of people who were converted in the revival in Britain passed one million out of a population of about twenty-seven million.

When I say that not all the Evangelicals were in favour, I'm thinking of one case in Bradford, West Yorkshire. The Anglicans and Free Churches got together and decided to have united meetings on Sunday night to try to win people to Christ. But the Anglicans had to have permission from the bishop to do so. The bishop of Ripon, by name Robert Bickersteth, was a Low Churchman, but he refused to give permission to have mixed meetings. He said he did not deny that the Free Church ministers such as Baptists, Methodists, and Congregationalists were servants of Jesus Christ according to their light, but they were not priests of the true church. He forbade any mixing.

So the Anglicans and Free Church people got together again wondering what they should do. Then someone came up with an idea. Why not have the first Sunday of the month under Anglican auspices? The Anglicans don't need permission to have an Anglican service. Then have the second service of the month Free Church. The Free Churches don't need the bishop's permission to have a meeting. And then the third Sunday would be Anglican, the fourth Sunday would be Free Church turnabout. The result was on certain Sundays they had the blessing of God and the benediction of the bishop, but on other Sundays only the blessing of God! They managed all right.

Now this revival spread throughout Britain and continued on in its effect in Europe. I have read a book written by a German scholar to say that the effect of that revival when it spread to Germany was thirty years of revival. The Scandinavian countries were affected also. Then on the mission fields, the revival was very effective in India. It stirred up the English-speaking people and also some of the Christian people in the south of India. A great revival began in 1860 in the southern extremity of India and spread throughout the Diocese of Tinnevelly. "Old and young, men, women, and children, were suddenly seen crushed by the agony of a deep conviction of sin, and then just as suddenly seemed to believe in the forgiveness of sins." That was written by an Anglican chaplain to his bishop.

I mentioned that in the revival in the United States there were no signs and wonders, such as tongues and healing. Neither could I find any in the 1859 movement in Great Britain. But when the movement reached India, there were dreams, and visions, and trances, and healings, and tongues, and interpretations—the whole thing. It's just enough to keep anyone from forming any kind of theory to explain the matter.

The revival was felt in other mission fields of the world, but perhaps I should explain that in certain other parts of the world there was a great impact of revival; for example, there was great movement in Australia. Most Australians ask me the question, "Why has dear old Australia never seen a great revival?" Well, they don't know the facts of their own history. When the news of the American revival came to Australia, some of the newspapers ridiculed it, and some warned against it; but Christian people began praying. A conference of ministers meeting in mid-1857 resolved to pray for general revival and revival for themselves, seeking a richer baptism of the Holy Spirit and promising to pray for each other and promote Saturday evening meetings for prayer.

Now the population of Australia at that time was just about one million and the concentrations of population were in Sydney and Melbourne. Towns were very small and churches were very small indeed. But the revival began through prayer meetings. Sydney editors reported a call for prayer. They said, "It would be a happy day for Sydney and New South Wales when a similar influence visits us here."

The extraordinary revival began in the town of Brighton, and before long, it spread to Melbourne itself, with great meetings in the city theatres following the London pattern. The Theatre Royale in Melbourne was crowded out

Sunday by Sunday. There were fifty thousand attending a dozen services. The congregations were very large and attentive, and yet regular worship services were not hurt in any way.

Revival spread to South Australia. The Reverend J.D. Wittaker, pastor in a town called Kooringa, announced, "Five hundred conversions in three months in the most glorious revival of religion, never such a one seen in this colony before." The Victorian Goldfields Revival Services were full of holy zeal and fire. Revival in Bendigo, and Ballarat, revival in Geelong; revival spread to other parts, to Tasmania, especially in the Tasmanian capital, Hobart, following a week of prayer conducted by Spencer Williams. There was a fifty percent increase in membership among the Tasmanian Methodists in a single year.

Then a most remarkable thing happened. William Taylor, who was known as "California Taylor," who had come out with the settlers at the time of the Gold Rush, was busy in the eastern United States during the 1858 revival. And after some ministry in the States, he made his way to Australia and got there in 1863. He became the great harvester of the revival, winning tens of thousands of people to Christ, most of whom joined the Methodists, but some other denominations. Those seven fruitful years in Australia showed an increase among the Anglicans of twenty-two percent; Presbyterians, twenty-five percent; Methodists, seventy-two percent; Congregationalists, twenty percent; Baptists, forty percent; and Lutherans, fifty-five percent, although that was partly due to German immigration after the Crimean War.

The revival spread to other parts of the South Seas. But the same revival had a great effect in South Africa. Now the South Africans heard of the revival from American missionaries coming back from Boston and other parts to their field in South Africa. But they were not too much impressed with news from America. They said to themselves, "Anything can happen over there." But when missionaries began to arrive from Scotland, telling of the Church of Scotland being in revival, they were deeply impressed and they started prayer meetings for revival in South Africa.

At Easter time, 1860, in a town called Worcester, about one hundred miles up-country from Capetown, there was a meeting of ministers, 137 gathered from all over the country, chiefly Dutch-speaking, but also some English-speaking. They heard the reports of the missionaries from the United States and the United Kingdom and they redoubled their prayer for revival in South Africa.

Seven weeks and one day later, at Whitson Tide on Whit Sunday, the celebration of Pentecost, the young Dutch Reformed people were having their youth meeting in the prayer hall near the Dutch Reformed Church at Worcester. A black girl, she was a Fingo girl, speaking the Xhosa language, got up to her feet and asked if she might give her testimony. The young man in charge, by name Johann Christian deVries, gave her permission. She gave such a sweet testimony; there was a hush of the sense of the presence of God. Then DeVries heard what he thought was an approaching tornado, and the whole prayer hall shook, he thought, and then all the young people were on their feet praying simultaneously, audibly.

Now Dutch Reformed people are not used to this. They're a very civil people. You could describe Dutch Reformed people as Presbyterians with a little extra starch! They were completely overwhelmed by this.

An elder was walking by; his name was Johann Rabe. He heard the commotion, went in to see what was happening and didn't like what he saw, so he rushed up to tell the minister. The minister came down right away, came in, and said unto DeVries, "What is happening?" He said something about the presence of God. The minister said, "I hold you responsible." He then spoke up and said, "[words spoken in Dutch]." "Everybody be quiet." Nobody took any notice. He said, "I am your minister sent by God. Will you be quiet?" They didn't even see him. He went back to DeVries and said, "Start a hymn." The two men started to sing in Dutch, but nobody joined them and the minister stomped out. He said, "God is a God of order. This is nothing but confusion!"

By the way, that minister was Andrew Murray. I didn't know Andrew Murray personally, but I knew his grandsons. I knew his biographer, and Oupa Douglas told me that Andrew Murray was a mellow old saint, three times Moderate of the Dutch Reformed Church, famous in the United States and the United Kingdom, famous as the author of many books. His friends used to tease him by saying, "Tell us, Dr. Murray, how you tried to stop the revival."

On Saturday night, he called a meeting in the schoolroom. More than one thousand people packed the place out. There were hundreds standing outside. He read the Scripture, gave a short commentary, then he said the meeting is now open for prayer. Again he heard the sound of an approaching tornado and then all one thousand people were on their feet praying simultaneously, audibly. A stranger outside forced his way in and touched Andrew Murray on the shoulder. He said in English, "Are you the minister of this congregation?" He replied that he was. He said, "Be careful what you do. This is the outpouring of the Holy Spirit." And that was the beginning of the greatest revival South Africa ever knew. Fifty young men out of that one parish entered the ministry, went to study at Stellenbosch, and the revival continued throughout the years.

Here's what G. W. A. Van der Lingen, who was a scholar and pastor at Paarl, said about enjoying the glory of the church in the first century: "After five years, the attendance has never been so good as in the year that has just passed. On many occasions, not only were all the seats and benches fully occupied, but people sat in the aisles and on the steps. Oft many people were turned away because they could not get a place."

William Taylor from Australia, came to South Africa, and began preaching to English-speaking people, and saw a most remarkable revival among the English-speaking whites. But the greatest work he did was among the black people of South

Africa, the Xhosa-speaking and the Zulu-speaking. He was a great preacher. He had a very wonderful interpreter, a Xhosa chief called Charles Pamla. He began preaching with this chief interpreting and they began having extraordinary meetings, sometimes as many as eight hundred converted in a single meeting.

How did they sum it up? The Methodists in London said, "After the lapse of more than half a century since Wesleyan missions were commenced in South Africa, a great and favourable change has taken place in the native work. There has been a glorious revival of religion in South Africa in the European and native populations."

It's impossible in the space allotted to tell what happened throughout the world in that revival. But one could sum it up by saying, "Wherever there was an Evangelical cause, there was revival. And wherever missionaries were preaching the Gospel, the old-time Gospel, there were phenomenal results." This was the 1859 revival throughout the Eastern hemisphere, just as the 1858 revival spread throughout the West.

The previous message was transcribed and reprinted with the permission of Mrs. Carol Orr.

Many of Dr. Orr's messages can be downloaded or reprinted, free of charge, by going to the following website:

www.jedwinorr.com

NOTES

Introduction

[1] *The Guardian Letters*, Professor Niall Shanks, East Tennessee State University, *Guardian Unlimited on the Web*, March 11, 2002. <http://www.guardian.co.uk/letters/story/0,3604,665237,00.html>, (February 20, 2003).

[2] A.C. Grayling. "The Last Word on Rationality." *Guardian Unlimited on the Web*. March 16, 2002. <http://www.guardian.co.uk/saturday_review/story/0,3605,668041,00.html>, (February 20, 2003).

[3] Tania Branigan. " 'Creationist' school has evolution debate." *Guardian Unlimited on the Web*, April 9, 2002. <http://www.guardian.co.uk/uk_news/story/0,3604,681133,00.html>, (February 20, 2003).

[4] Matthew Parris. "There's God's Way, Darwin's Way - and the Third Way." *The Times on the Web,* March 16, 2002. <http://www.newsint-archive.co.uk>, (April 15, 2003).

Chapter One

[5] Keith J. Hardman. *The Spiritual Awakeners.* Moody Press, Chicago, Illinois, 1983, p. 112.

[6] Ibid.

[7] Thomas Paine. *Age of Reason.* US History webpage, <<u>http://www.ushistory.org/paine/reason/reason3.htm</u>>, (April 15, 2003).

[8] Elihu Palmer. *Principles of Nature.* Reproduced by Steve Dowell and Jay Boswell from a photocopy of the original 1819 text. October, 2002. <<u>http://www.deistnet.com/princnat.htm</u>>, (April 15, 2003).

[9] Ibid.

[10] J. Edwin Orr. "The Role of Prayer in Spiritual Awakenings." Oxford Association for Research in Revival, Los Angeles, California, 1976, p. 1.

[11] Ibid, p. 2.

[12] Ibid.

[13] Ibid, p. 3.

Chapter Two

[14] Richard W. DeHaan. *How to Have Revival.* Radio Bible Class, Grand Rapids, Michigan, 1984, pp. 2–3.

[15] Keith J. Hardman. *The Spiritual Awakeners.* Moody Press, Chicago, Illinois, 1983, p. 21.

[16] Ibid, p. 20.

Chapter Three

[17] A.W. Tozer. *The Pursuit of God.* Christian Publications, Inc., Camp Hill, Pennsylvania, 1982, 1993, p. 66.

Chapter Four

[18] J. Edwin Orr. *The Flaming Tongue.* Moody Press, Chicago, Illinois, 1973, p. 3.

Chapter Five

[19] Barna Research Group, 5528 Everglades, Ventura, CA 93003. www.barna.org. http://www.barna.org/cgi-bin/pagepressrelease.asp?pressreleaseID=97&reference=B.

[20] J. Edwin Orr. "The Role of Prayer in Spiritual Awakenings." Oxford Association for Research in Revival, Los Angeles, California, 1976, pp. 4–5.

[21] Missionary Standard. Author, date, and publisher unknown.

Chapter Six

[22] Matthew Henry. (from *Matthew Henry's Commentary on the Whole Bible*: New Modern Edition, Electronic Database. Copyright © 1991 by Hendrickson Publishers, Inc.) [commenting on Zechariah 12:9].

About the Author

Brian Brodersen has been involved in pastoral ministry since 1981. He served as senior pastor of Calvary Chapel Vista, California, and also as senior pastor of Calvary Chapel Westminster, London, England.

Brian has been extensively involved in missionary work throughout Europe. He now serves as associate pastor to Chuck Smith at Calvary Chapel Costa Mesa, California.

Brian is the featured speaker on the Bible teaching program "Back to Basics." He is best known for his clear and challenging exposition of the Scriptures.

Brian and his wife Cheryl have four children and one grandson, and reside in Southern California.

For program information or to obtain other teaching materials by Pastor Brian, you may call 800.733.6443 or go to the "Back to Basics" website:

www.calvarybasics.com